American Politics Today

Lobbyists and Special Interest Groups

Elisabeth Herschbach

ELDORADO INK

Eldorado Ink
PO Box 100097
Pittsburgh, PA 15233
www.eldoradoink.com

Produced by OTTN Publishing, Stockton, New Jersey

CPSIA compliance information: Batch#MAP2016.
For further information, contact Eldorado Ink at info@eldoradoink.com.

First printing

1 3 5 7 9 8 6 4 2

Library of Congress Cataloging-in-Publication Data

Names: Herschbach, Elisabeth.
Title: Lobbyists and special interest groups / by Elisabeth Herschbach.
Description: Pittsburgh, PA : Eldorado Ink, [2016] | Series: American
  politics today | Includes bibliographical references and index.
Identifiers: LCCN 2015048674 (print) | LCCN 2016002073 (ebook) | ISBN
  9781619000902 (hc) | ISBN 9781619000988 (pb) | ISBN 9781619001060 (trade)
  | ISBN 9781619001145 (ebook)
Subjects: LCSH: Lobbyists—Juvenile literature. | Pressure groups—Juvenile literature.
Classification: LCC JK1118 .H44 2016 (print) | LCC JK1118 (ebook) | DDC
  324/.40973—dc23
LC record available at http://lccn.loc.gov/2015048674

For information about custom editions, special sales, or premiums,
please contact our special sales department at info@eldoradoink.com.

Table of Contents

Chapter 1

What's So Special about Special Interests?

On July 20, 2012, a gunman opened fire in a movie theater in Aurora, Colorado, killing twelve people and wounding fifty-eight. Five months later, twenty students and six adults were gunned down at Sandy Hook Elementary School in Newtown, Connecticut. That was the deadliest school shooting in U.S. history.

These high-profile tragedies put gun violence in the national spotlight. Support for gun control legislation exploded, both among the general public and among lawmakers. Several states considered proposals to strengthen existing gun laws. On the federal level, a bipartisan proposal to expand background checks on gun purchases was introduced in the Senate. It was called the Manchin-Toomey Background Checks bill, after its Senate sponsors.

Polls showed that 90 percent of Americans supported universal background checks. Four months after the Newtown shooting, however, the Manchin-Toomey bill was defeated in the Senate by a slim mar-

K Street has become a nickname for the lobbying industry. It refers to a street in downtown Washington, D.C., where many lobbying firms have their offices.

gin. A disappointed President Barack Obama blamed the "gun lobby and its allies" for the defeat. A minority of senators, he complained, put the interests of the National Rifle Association (NRA) above the will of their constituents.

Politicians of all stripes regularly voice similar complaints. When President Obama vetoed a controversial pipeline project to carry oil from Canada to Texas, Republican Senate Majority Leader Mitch McConnell denounced the decision as "a victory for partisanship and for powerful special interests." On the other side of the aisle, Democratic senator Chuck Schumer said that Republicans pushing for the pipeline were just trying to appease "a few special interests, in this case, oil companies and pipeline companies."

The view that special interests are ruining American government is so widespread, in fact, that it has become a common campaign rallying cry. Republican presidential candidate Rand Paul launched his 2016 bid for the White House by proclaiming, "We have come to take our country back from the special interests that use Washington as their personal piggy bank, the special interests that are more concerned with their personal welfare than the general welfare."

Who and what are these lobbyists and special interests that everyone wants to blame for all the failings of our political process?

INTEREST GROUPS BIG AND SMALL

Special-interest groups—also simply called interest groups—are organized groups of people who share a common interest, perspective, or policy goal that they collectively promote through the political process. The best-known examples are powerful, highly active organizations like the NRA, which have millions of members and multimillion-dollar budgets and make it into the news hundreds of times a year. But interest groups come in all sizes and shapes, and groups representing just about every conceivable issue and point of view are found across the American political landscape.

Some groups focus on economic interests. Business organizations, including corporations like ExxonMobil, Boeing, and Procter & Gamble, shell out big bucks to promote their economic interests in

Demonstrators in Los Angeles protest against the influence of money in American politics. Lobbyists and interest groups are often blamed for gridlock in the American political system, or for legislation that favors the wealthy over "regular" people.

government. Labor unions, trade associations, and professional associations also represent economic interests—specifically, the economic interests of people engaged in certain trades, industries, and professions.

The American Bar Association is one of the largest professional associations in the United States. It supports the interests of practicing lawyers and sets professional standards for the field. Well-known trade associations include the American Petroleum Institute, which represents oil companies; the National Association of Wheat Growers; and the National Cattlemen's Beef Association. Just about every industry has its own trade association, no matter how obscure. The National Frozen Pizza Institute, for example, promotes the interests of

Members of a teacher's union demonstrate in Chicago. Members of labor unions pay annual dues, some of which are used to lobby government leaders to pass legislation that is aligned with the interests of union workers.

makers of frozen pizzas. The Balloon Council represents retailers, distributors, and manufacturers of balloons.

Trade associations represent groups of businesses in a particular trade or industry. Labor unions, by contrast, represent the interests of the workers themselves. Unions advocate for better wages and working conditions for workers in specific industries. One of the best known is the International Brotherhood of Teamsters, which represents transportation workers. Teachers, autoworkers, steelworkers, and service employees also have their own unions, as do many other types of workers.

CITIZEN GROUPS AND PUBLIC INTEREST GROUPS

In addition to groups with an economic focus, there are also hundreds of interest groups working to promote various social, political, or civic causes. These include church groups and religious organizations, social justice groups, environmental organizations, and civil rights groups, among others. Because these types of groups are open to any citizen who identifies with the cause, they are often referred to as "citizen groups." Prominent citizen groups include the American Civil Liberties Association, the National Wildlife Federation, and the Christian Coalition.

Some organizations are known as single-issue groups because they focus on a single policy area, such as abortion or gun control. Others

Special, or Not?

The expression *special interest* is sometimes thought to be a loaded term, conveying an implicit criticism of a group's role in the political process. President Obama articulates this negative connotation in his political memoir *The Audacity of Hope*:

> I've never been entirely comfortable with the term "special interest," which lumps together ExxonMobil and bricklayers; the pharmaceutical lobby and the parents of special-ed kids . . . [T]o my mind, there's a difference between a corporate lobby whose clout is based on money alone, and a group of like-minded individuals—whether they be textile workers, gun aficionados, veterans, or family farmers—coming together to promote their interests; between those who use their economic power to magnify their political influence far beyond what their numbers might justify, and those who are simply seeking to pool their votes to sway their representatives. The former subvert the very idea of democracy. The latter are its essence.

Because of this perceived negative connotation, some political scientists and commentators prefer to use the more neutral terms *interest group* or *organized interests*.

work on a range of issues from a particular ideological point of view. The National Organization for Women, for example, addresses a variety of issues from a feminist perspective. The Family Research Council represents a conservative, Christian point of view. Some interest groups—known as public interest groups—concentrate on issues that are of wider public concern, such as consumer rights, health advocacy, and education.

LOBBYISTS: A FOURTH BRANCH OF GOVERNMENT?

Interest groups do many things. They provide policymakers, clients, and the general public with information relevant to their mission. Their representatives make statements to the media. They monitor legislation on issues that affect their interests. They collect data on constituents' views and conduct research related to their spheres of action. If they are membership organizations, they provide services to their members. If they are cause-oriented groups, they mobilize support for their cause among the general public.

The specific things an interest group does may vary, depending on the type of group it is. To some degree or another, however, all interest groups engage in lobbying.

Lobbying refers to the attempt to influence government policies in a certain way. We sometimes use the term loosely to describe any political advocacy efforts. In this loose sense, any time you sign a petition or write a letter to Congress to voice your opinion on a political

According to a popular political legend, Ulysses S. Grant invented the term lobbyist to refer to favor-seekers congregating in the lobby of the Willard Hotel during his tenure as president of the United States (1869–1877). According to most historians, however, the term actually originated in the House of Commons in seventeenth-century England, where constituents used to wait to petition members of parliament in the foyers, or lobbies, of the building.

Officers of the Hope and Grace Initiative present a $75,000 check to the National Alliance on Mental Illness, a lobbying firm that works to raise awareness of matters related to mental health. During 2015 the National Alliance on Mental Illness was working to get Congress to pass two bills in the House of Representatives and one in the U.S. Senate.

issue, you are lobbying. Typically, however, we use the word in a more restricted sense to describe political advocacy undertaken specifically on behalf of interest groups.

A lobbyist in this sense is a professional who represents an interest group in the political arena. Some lobbyists, called contract lobbyists, work for lobbying firms that take on many different interest groups as clients. Most lobbyists, however, work in-house for a specific association or organization. In either case, the job of a lobbyist is to try to shape public policy in a way that favors a particular group's agenda.

Lobbyists are involved in just about every political decision at every level of government. They lobby Congress and the White House, federal agencies and state governments, city councils and school boards. They raise money, run ads, and mobilize voters in elections. They file lawsuits to achieve their goals through litigation. They testify at congressional hearings and hold face-to-face meetings with government officials. They may even draft legislation. Lobbyists are so influential and so central to every stage of the political process that they are sometimes referred to as a fourth branch of government, alongside the legislative, executive, and judicial branches.

POWER AND PARADOX

The right to form interest groups and to lobby the government is guaranteed under the First Amendment of the U.S. Constitution, which states that "Congress shall make no law abridging the freedom of speech or of the press, or the right of the people to peaceably assemble, and to petition the government for a redress of grievances."

Lobbyists and interest groups, however, occupy a paradoxical place in American politics. On the one hand, most Americans seem to share the cynical view about them expressed by President Obama in his remarks on gun control and Senator Rand Paul in his campaign speech. Seventy-one percent of respondents in a 2011 Gallup poll, for example, complained that lobbyists have too much power in government. In a 2015 survey conducted by the Pew Research Center, 74 percent of respondents agreed that "most elected officials put their own interests ahead of the country." Just 3% of Americans said they can trust the government in Washington to do what is right "just about always."

On the other hand, most Americans—as many as 80 percent, according to some estimates—belong to at least one organization that fits the definition of an interest group. For many Americans, joining an interest group is an important way to participate in the political process. Historically, many of the social benefits we take for granted—including civil rights laws, child labor restrictions, and other workplace regulations—were won in part through the lobbying efforts of interest groups.

Chapter 2

Lobbyists and Special Interests

Lobbyists and interest groups have been a fixture in American politics since the early days of the nation. One of the first recorded instances of lobbying was in 1792, when veterans of the Continental Army hired a former Revolutionary War officer named William Hull to lobby the newly formed Congress for additional money in compensation for their service during the war. Several of today's most influential groups have histories stretching back to the years right after the Civil War. The NRA, for example, was formed in 1871. The American Bankers Association dates to 1875.

But although lobbyists and special-interest groups are not a recent phenomenon, what is new is the scale of their involvement in contemporary politics. Today, there are more interest groups in the United States than ever before, and these groups are spending unprecedented amounts of money to promote their agendas in government.

AN EXPLOSION OF INTEREST GROUPS

According to scholars, the number of interest groups active across the country grew exponentially in the 1960s and early 1970s. This trend has continued into the twenty-first century. In 1970, there were an estimated 4,000 or so Washington-based interest groups. Today, conservative estimates put the number at as many as 20,000 groups in Washington alone. Nationwide, the number of interest groups in operation today is thought to be well over 200,000.

As interest groups have proliferated, they have also become increasingly diverse. Historically, trade associations, professional associations, and labor unions constituted the majority of interest groups. More recently, however, there has been what some political scientists call an "advocacy explosion"—a proliferation of citizen groups and cause-oriented advocacy groups lobbying for social change. These groups focus their efforts on an ever-expanding roster of issues, ranging from consumer protection to animal rights to same-sex marriage. Interestingly, religious interest groups have increased at a higher rate than secular groups. Over the past four decades, the number of religious groups active in the nation has grown roughly fivefold, from approximately 40 groups in 1970 to more than 200 today.

LOBBYISTS BY THE NUMBERS

In line with the explosive growth in interest groups, the number of lobbyists has also skyrocketed. Today, there are more than 11,000 registered lobbyists in the nation's capital alone—nearly 22 lobbyists for every member of Congress. Not included in that figure are the thousands of unregistered lobbyists who are not on the books. According to some estimates, the actual number of lobbyists working in Washington—registered and unregistered—is closer to 25,000. That comes to about one federal lobbyist for every twenty-six D.C. residents.

Outside of Washington, there are thousands of additional lobbyists working at the state and local level. For example, in 2012 there were 5,700 registered lobbyists in New York and 3,500 registered lobbyists in Illinois. Texas and Ohio each counted over 1,500 registered lobbyists in 2012.

Every year, these lobbyists spend billions of dollars trying to shape the outcome of public policy decisions at every level of government. At the federal level alone, lobbyists collectively spent $3.24 billion in 2014, according to the Center for Responsive Politics. By comparison,

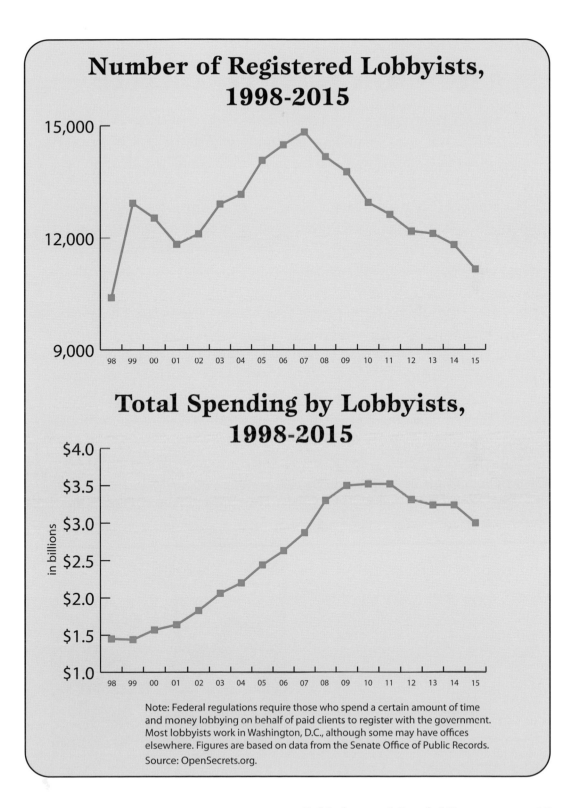

Number of Registered Lobbyists, 1998-2015

Total Spending by Lobbyists, 1998-2015

in billions

Note: Federal regulations require those who spend a certain amount of time and money lobbying on behalf of paid clients to register with the government. Most lobbyists work in Washington, D.C., although some may have offices elsewhere. Figures are based on data from the Senate Office of Public Records.
Source: OpenSecrets.org.

The Obamacare Battle

The Patient Protection and Affordable Care Act, enacted on March 23, 2010, was the most significant attempt to reform the U.S. health care system since the 1960s. It was also the most hotly contested piece of legislation in modern U.S. history.

Hundreds of lobbyists campaigned for or against the legislation—colloquially called "Obamacare"—on behalf of hundreds of groups with a stake in the issue. Not surprisingly, medical associations, insurance companies, and pharmaceutical companies were the heaviest hitters. But a wide range of other organizations also sent lobbyists to Capitol Hill to weigh in on just about every specific detail of the 2,700-page bill, as well as over 10,000 pages of regulations related to the Affordable Care Act. These groups included labor unions, business groups, religious organizations, manufacturing associations, and food and beverage companies. Even Dunkin' Donuts entered the fight. According to Senate lobbying records, the popular doughnut chain lobbied against a proposal to implement a soda tax to help pay for health care reform.

In total, 1,750 different corporations and organizations reported lobbying on Obamacare in 2009. The biggest spender opposed to health care reform was the U.S. Chamber of Commerce, which shelled out $65 million in 2009 to lobby against Obamacare. Hospitals and nursing homes coughed up $77 million lobbying to support it. Collectively, interest groups on both sides of the issue spent a record-setting $600 million in a single year. That figure doesn't include the additional millions spent on TV commercials—over $160 million in 2009, according to the Campaign Media Analysis Group.

the total was $1.57 billion in 2000. By industry sector, the top spender in 2014 was the pharmaceutical industry: Pharmaceutical lobbyists spent almost $300 million on lobbying. In 2014, business associations collectively spent more than $160 million. Oil and gas companies lobbied to the tune of more than $140 million.

FACTIONS, PLURALISM, AND DEMOCRACY

Worries about the influence of interest groups are as old as the groups themselves. In the Federalist Papers, written in 1787, founding father James Madison warned about the dangers of what he called "factions"—groups of citizens "united and actuated by some common impulse of passion, or of interest, adverse to the rights of other citizens." He wrote that factions—that is, interest groups—are the chief cause of political conflict and instability because these groups promote their own interests at the expense of the common good.

In Madison's view, however, the solution is not for government to limit the formation of interest groups. Because the right of association is a vital part of self-expression, that would be a remedy "worse than the disease." Moreover, Madison felt limiting groups would be counterproductive. He believed the solution is to promote a political system that actually encourages more groups to form. According to Madison, these diverse groups will compete against each other, creating a system of checks and balances. Competition among these groups will prevent any single group from growing too strong.

The view that democracy is based on a shifting balance among competing groups is known as pluralism. According to this view, both interest groups and lobbyists are part of a healthy democracy. They are the primary way in which citizens participate in the democratic process. Given the diversity of the United States, no elected official can effectively represent the wide-ranging interests, needs, and priorities of all constituents. People who share a specific set of concerns can mobilize to safeguard and promote their interests by forming groups. These groups give citizens a collective voice in the political process, and lobbyists push for that voice to be represented in government.

INTEREST GROUPS AND GRIDLOCK

Many political scientists today share this positive view of the role of interest groups in American government. Some critics, however, are not convinced that the proliferation of interest groups is a healthy thing for democracy.

One common criticism is that the sheer number of groups involved in the political process today makes it nearly impossible for the government to get anything done. This idea is sometimes referred to as hyperpluralism.

According to this view, there are so many different groups pushing so many different agendas that lawmakers become caught in a gridlock of competing interests. Every piece of legislation involves so many compromises and so many concessions made to powerful special interests that the final product has no impact at all. This, then, weakens government because it loses the ability to enact needed laws. For some critics, a glaring example of this inability to act is the failure of Congress to pass climate change legislation, even in the face of mounting evidence of the urgent need to do so.

Other critics argue that the problem is not that government can't get anything done. It's that government decisions are biased in favor of the wealthiest elements in society. According to these critics, big money is hijacking the democratic process, giving wealthier groups greater leverage and clout in politics.

FOLLOW THE MONEY

Although there are more interest groups in America than ever before, not all of these groups enjoy equal stature. Interest groups represent-

Although most people think of the Girl Scouts and the Boy Scouts exclusively as youth groups, both organizations have an active lobbying wing. The Girl Scouts of America spent almost a quarter of a million dollars in 2014 lobbying on at least ten different pieces of legislation in Congress.

Lobbyists seek to influence state and local government leaders, not just federal legislators. These people are demonstrating on the steps of the Utah State Capitol building, demanding that the state government do something about air pollution in Salt Lake City.

ing social or political viewpoints, for example, are far less influential than groups representing economic interests. And among groups representing economic interests, corporations are much more prominent than unions.

Compared to all other types of organizations, corporations and business groups engage in the greatest amount of lobbying every year, and they spend the most money doing so. Depending on the estimate, corporations and trade associations are responsible for up to 84 percent of all money spent on lobbying in a given year.

The pro-business U.S. Chamber of Commerce, for example, spent a staggering $124 million on lobbying efforts in 2014, making it the top spender of the year. By comparison, the Teamsters union spent slightly over $2 million in 2014. The NAACP, one of the nation's most prominent civil rights organizations, spent less than half a million dollars on lobbying. The National Children's Alliance spent $78,000, and the Disability Rights and Education Fund spent just under $18,000.

Lobbyists for the oil and gas industry spend hundreds of millions of dollars each year to protect corporate interests. According to data from the Senate Office of Public Records, in 2015 ExxonMobil spent more than $9.1 million on lobbying efforts, followed by Koch Industries ($7.6 million) and Royal Dutch Shell ($6.5 million). The American Petroleum Institute, a trade association that represents oil and natural gas companies, spent over $6 million in 2015.

On just about any given issue, business groups outspend other interest groups. In 2009, for example, environmental groups collectively spent $22.4 million in support of climate change legislation—legislation that was ultimately defeated in the Senate. This was a record amount of money for these groups—more than twice their average annual expenditures for 2000–2008. The oil and gas industry, however, shelled out a staggering $175 million to lobby against climate change legislation. That's almost eight times as much as the environmental groups spent. The oil company ExxonMobil alone spent $27.4 million on lobbying during that period—more than all of the environmental groups combined.

WATCHDOG GROUPS AND PUBLIC OVERSIGHT

Critics raise important concerns about the impact of lobbying dollars on the political process. Clearly, there are deep inequalities in the resources that different interest groups have to promote their point of view through lobbying. It is less clear, however, how much of an impact this has on policymaking. According to most researchers, it is hard to demonstrate a consistent pattern between the amount of money spent by lobbyists on different sides of an issue and the eventual policy outcome.

There does seem to be evidence, however, that lobbying can buy other types of perks for organizations. For example, corporations that lobby seem to win more government contracts, pay lower taxes, and encounter fewer problems with regulatory agencies than corporations that do not lobby.

Either way, just about everyone agrees that oversight is important. Unless lobbying is done in a transparent, publicly accessible way, it is hard to ensure accountability. The late Robert Byrd, the longest-serving U.S. senator, put it this way:

> Congress has always had, and always will have, lobbyists and lobbying. . . . At the same time, the history of this institution demonstrates the need for eternal vigilance to ensure that lobbyists do not abuse their role, that lobbying is carried on publicly with full publicity, and that the interests of all citizens are heard without giving special ear to the best organized and most lavishly funded.

A number of government watchdog groups, including the Center for Responsive Politics and the Sunlight Foundation, are dedicated to promoting this kind of oversight. They maintain extensive, public databases that track and publicize the money trail of lobbyists in American politics. This information is available to the public because of lobbying regulations passed by Congress in the past twenty years.

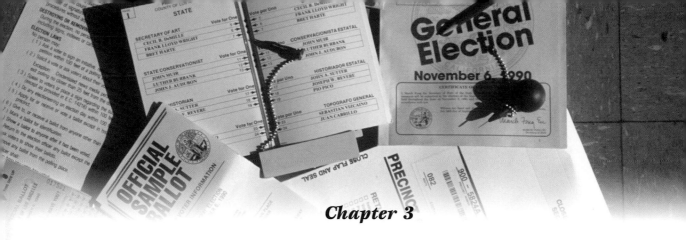

Chapter 3

Regulation and Reform

Lobbyists pay (and are paid) big money to try to influence law-makers and other public officials. Given the amount of money involved and the potential for bias and corruption, it is not surprising that some people are uneasy about the practice. Yet lobbying is a legitimate part of the political process, protected by the First Amendment. As we saw in chapter 1, interest group formation is an expression of the right to assemble. Lobbying is an expression of the right to petition the government.

Because lobbying is protected under the Constitution, lawmakers have steered clear of heavy restrictions aimed at curbing the practice. Instead, regulations have focused on promoting transparency—in other words, making sure that lobbying activities are aboveboard and in the open. Lobbying regulations at both the state and federal level aim to provide this transparency by requiring lobbyists to register and to disclose their activities.

The rationale behind these regulations is that the public is entitled

There are sixteen lobbyists representing corporate interests for every one lobbyist representing a labor union or public-interest group.

Congressman Alfred Phillips proudly shows off a sign on his office door that indicates his refusal to be swayed by paid lobbyists, 1938. Concerns over the influence of corporate and union funds in Congress led to passage of the Federal Regulation of Lobbying Act of 1946.

to know who the lobbyists are, what issues they are concerned with, what specific positions they are advocating, and how much money they are spending on lobbying. After all, the decisions made by lawmakers affect all citizens, either directly or indirectly. It stands to reason, then, that the public has a right to know how lawmakers reach their decisions. That includes having access to information about the potential influence of lobbyists.

EARLY ATTEMPTS AT LOBBYING REFORM

Attempts to regulate federal lobbying date back to 1876, when the House of Representatives passed a short-lived resolution requiring lobbyists to register with the clerk of the House. Congress passed the first comprehensive federal lobbying law just after World War II. The Federal Regulation of Lobbying Act of 1946 required anyone or any group whose "principal purpose" was to influence legislation in Congress to register with the clerk of the House. It also required lobbyists to file periodic financial reports itemizing their earnings and expenditures.

Thanks to significant loopholes, however, the legislation was widely regarded as ineffective. For example, the scope of the law was too narrow. It applied only to lobbying efforts directed at legislators and not congressional staff or executive branch officials. The definition of terms was also too vague to be useful. The legislation offered no concrete measure specifying whether lobbying was an individual or an organization's "principal purpose." As a result, it was unclear exactly to whom the registration and reporting requirements applied. Finally, the legislation did not include any effective mechanism for evaluating the accuracy of lobbyists' reports or for prosecuting violations.

THE LOBBYING DISCLOSURE ACT OF 1995

Congress attempted to address these weaknesses half a century later with the Lobbying Disclosure Act of 1995 (LDA). The LDA introduced several key improvements, aimed at promoting a greater degree of transparency and accountability in federal lobbying practices.

For example, the legislation strengthened registration and disclosure requirements, mandating that lobbyists file reports twice a year disclosing what issues they are lobbying on and how much they are spending. The LDA also clarified the definition of lobbying activities to eliminate vagueness and ambiguity. It extended the scope of the law to include lobbying directed at congressional staff and members of the executive branch. Importantly, the legislation also introduced a quantifiable threshold for when the registration and reporting requirements kick in.

Specifically, it stipulated that individuals are required to disclose their lobbying activities and to register with the clerk of the House and the secretary of the Senate if they meet all three of the following conditions: (1) They directly contact a lawmaker or staff member more than once, (2) they make more than $3,000 from lobbying over

Wisconsin Congressman Carl Levin sponsored legislation in the U.S. Senate that was eventually passed as the Lobbying Disclosure Act of 1995.

a three-month period, and (3) they spend at least 20 percent of their time lobbying for a single client.

LOOPHOLES AND SHORTCOMINGS

The Lobbying Disclosure Act of 1995 was the most comprehensive political ethics and lobbying reform bill ever passed at the federal

Lobbying Reform in the Fifty States

The Lobbying Disclosure Act of 1995 and the Honest Leadership and Open Government Act of 2007 apply only to lobbying at the federal level. Currently, however, all fifty states have their own lobbying regulations, with various degrees of strictness. All states require lobbyists to register and to report their activities. Many states, including Colorado, Florida, and North Carolina, also ban gifts to lawmakers. Wisconsin is widely heralded as one of the states with the most effective disclosure laws. Under Wisconsin regulations, lobbyists and the organizations they represent are required to register after just five conversations with lawmakers and to identify the position they lobbied for. Moreover, all lobbying data is available online in a sortable and searchable database.

As with federal lobbying laws, state reforms have often been inspired by major lobbying scandals. For example, California tightened its gift restrictions in 1990 following the so-called Shrimpscam scandal in the late 1980s. Over the course of a three-year sting operation, FBI agents posed as lobbyists for a bogus shrimp-processing company and offered bribes to California lawmakers in exchange for votes. Three state legislators were convicted. Similarly, Arizona strengthened its lobbying regulations after a 1991 scandal in which seven state legislators were caught on camera taking bribes in exchange for supporting legislation to legalize casino gambling in the state.

level. It represented a major improvement over the requirements set by the previous Federal Regulation of Lobbying Act of 1946. Yet the LDA also had a number of shortcomings.

No single agency was put in charge of enforcing LDA provisions. Instead, the offices of the clerk of the House and the secretary of the Senate each maintained records separately. In addition, these offices lacked both the authority to enforce the regulations and the resources for monitoring compliance. The fact that lobbyists filed their financial reports in paper format, rather than electronically, also hindered oversight and transparency. Without a searchable, sortable electronic database of records, public access to information was severely limited.

The LDA failed to address certain lobbying practices that raise ethical concerns, including gift giving, campaign contributions, and the so-called "revolving door" issue. This is the colloquial term for the widespread practice of former public officials going on to take high-paid lobbying jobs after leaving office. The revolving door is controversial because it raises the concern that former officials are able to use their powerful connections and clout to gain undue influence for special-interest groups.

Finally, the 20 percent lobbying threshold opened up a significant loophole. Lobbyists could avoid registering and filing lobbying reports simply by ensuring that their lobbying activities for a given client fell short of the 20 percent threshold. This exemption clause is sometimes dubbed the "Daschle loophole" after former U.S. Senator Tom Daschle, a Democrat from South Dakota. For a decade after leaving Congress, Daschle enjoyed a lucrative lobbying career but never registered as a lobbyist or disclosed his lobbying activities. Instead of calling himself a lobbyist, he called himself a "strategic policy adviser." In March 2015, Daschle finally registered as a lobbyist because of work he was doing on behalf of the Republic of Taiwan.

Tom Daschle

Newt Gingrich

Daschle is by no means the only well-known influence peddler in Washington to take advantage of this loophole. Former Speaker of the House Newt Gingrich, a Republican from Georgia, has also made millions as a "policy historian" and "consultant" since leaving Congress, but has never registered as a lobbyist or filed a lobbying report.

THE ABRAMOFF SCANDAL AND LOBBYING REFORM

The Lobbying Disclosure Act of 1995 was in large part inspired by the Wedtech scandal, a high-profile corruption case that shook Congress in the late 1980s. Lobbyists for the Wedtech Corporation won lucra-

Jack Abramoff, a well-connected Washington lobbyist, leaves a federal courthouse in Miami after his indictment on corruption charges. In January 2006, Abramoff was sentenced to six years in federal prison for mail fraud, conspiracy to bribe public officials, and tax evasion.

tive government contracts through questionable means, including unreported lobbying activities and even bribery. The scandal implicated as many as twenty government officials at the state, local, and federal levels and shed light on the inadequacy of federal lobbying laws at the time.

Similarly, another high-profile lobbying scandal served as the impetus for Congress to address some of the shortcomings of the LDA. In this case, the scandal involved a high-powered Washington lobbyist named Jack Abramoff, who was convicted in 2006 of fraud, tax evasion, and conspiracy to bribe public officials. In connection with the Abramoff case, Representative Bob Ney, a Republican of Ohio, was also sentenced for taking bribes.

Bribery and corruption, of course, were never considered legitimate lobbying practices. We don't need lobbying laws to outlaw such practices. They are already illegal under criminal law.

The Abramoff corruption scandal, however, put public pressure on Congress to show that lobbying reform was a political priority. Congress responded by passing new lobbying reform measures in 2007.

HONEST LEADERSHIP AND OPEN GOVERNMENT

The Honest Leadership and Open Government Act (HLOGA) was signed into law on September 15, 2007. Although it does not close the so-called Daschle loophole, the legislation amends other parts of the Lobbying Disclosure Act.

The legislation requires lobbyists to file reports every three months, instead of twice a year. It also expands the amount of infor-

Hollywood brought the Abramoff scandal to the silver screen in the 2010 movie *Casino Jack*, starring Kevin Spacey. Also released in 2010 was a documentary film about the scandal called *Casino Jack and the United States of Money*, directed by Alex Gibney.

John D. Podesta, pictured here speaking with the media in 2015, is one of many Washington insiders who regularly shift between paid lobbying for clients and government service. Podesta served as Chief of Staff for President Bill Clinton (1998-2001) and as Counselor for President Barack Obama (2014-2015); in 2003, he founded the Center for American Progress, a major liberal advocacy organization. His lobbying business, the Podesta Group, earned over $17 million in 2015 lobbying for the government of Puerto Rico and for dozens of major firms like Wells Fargo bank, the defense contractor Lockheed Martin, and retail chain Walmart.

mation that lobbyists are required to report. Under the HLOGA, registered lobbyists are required to disclose not just lobbying activities but also campaign contributions and requests for congressional earmarks.

In an effort to improve transparency, the legislation established an electronic filing system for lobbying reports. All data is now fully downloadable from a searchable, sortable online database. And in an effort to promote accountability and enforceability, the HLOGA requires annual audits by the Government Accountability Office and increases penalties for violators.

In addition to boosting disclosure regulations, the Honest Leadership and Open Government Act also bolsters ethics regulations.

With some exceptions—including gifts under $5—the legislation bans lobbyists from giving gifts to lawmakers. Gift giving has always been controversial in the public's eye; it is associated with the negative stereotype of the wealthy "hired gun" trying to buy politicians with favors.

The HLOGA also makes it illegal for members of Congress to help people get jobs in the private sector based on political affiliation. This change was in response to a scandal surrounding the so-called K Street Project, an effort launched in 1995 by Republican strategist Grover Norquist and former House Majority Leader Tom DeLay, a Republican from Texas. The K Street Project pressured Washington lobbying firms to hire Republicans and fire Democrats by promising them special access to influential government officials.

LOBBYING IN THE SHADOWS

Unlike the LDA, the HLOGA addresses the issue of the revolving door. Among other measures designed to slow the flow from Capital Hill to K Street, the legislation prohibits members of Congress and executive branch officials from lobbying for two years after leaving office.

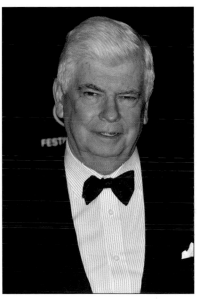

According to many experts, however, these prohibitions have been a mixed blessing. Because the HLOGA retains the same threshold requirements, it is still just as easy for lobbyists to claim exemption from the registration requirements. The new revolving door provisions simply add an extra incentive for lobbyists to take advantage of this loophole and remain unregistered.

Critics point to a noticeable decrease in the number of lobbyists registered since

Between 1998 and 2011, 79 percent of former members of Congress went on to take lobbying jobs, with an average annual income of $2 million. One of the more well-known revolving door lobbyists is former senator Chris Dodd, who now works for the Motion Picture Association of America.

2008 as evidence of this growing trend. Some refer to these unregistered lobbyists as "shadow lobbyists." Because unregistered lobbyists do not file disclosure reports, the rise of shadow lobbying is an obvious obstacle to promoting transparency in lobbying.

WHITE HOUSE LOBBYING REFORMS

President Barack Obama took a tough stance on lobbying from the beginning of his presidency. On January 21, 2009—the day after his inauguration—President Obama issued an executive order aimed at strengthening ethics regulations at the executive level of government. The executive order barred registered lobbyists from serving on advisory committees or working on issues they had previously lobbied on. It also prohibited those who have been registered as lobbyists within the preceding two years from being appointed to any executive agencies they had lobbied within that two-year period. These provisions were tightened in a second executive order issued in 2010.

By September 2009, however, about a dozen special waivers had already been granted to former lobbyists, allowing them to take positions in the administration. This has led to criticisms of backpedaling. Critics have also argued that the Obama administration's crackdown on hiring former lobbyists has simply introduced yet another disincentive for lobbyists to register, further promoting shadow lobbying.

Chapter 4

Interest Groups and Elections

Interest groups hire lobbyists as a means of shaping public policy. By lobbying elected officials, interest groups hope to affect the decisions these officials make. But another way that they try to shape public policy is by exerting influence over who gets elected in the first place. In other words, interest groups use election campaigns as a way to try to reshape government itself. Instead of simply trying to bring existing lawmakers around to their point of view, in the case of electoral lobbying, interest groups try to bring officials to power who are already sympathetic to their point of view.

Interest groups participate in elections in many different ways. They endorse specific candidates, recruit their own candidates, distribute voter guides, register voters, and organize get-out-the-vote initiatives. Controversially, they also spend increasing amounts of money on campaign contributions and election-related advertising.

THE FEDERAL ELECTION CAMPAIGN ACT

Concerns about the potentially damaging effects of big money on elections date back to the beginning of the twentieth century. In 1907,

Congress banned corporations and banks from making direct contributions to candidates when it passed the Tillman Act. The ban was extended to labor unions with the Taft-Hartley Act of 1947.

These laws were superseded by the Federal Election Campaign Act (FECA) of 1971, which became the backbone of our modern campaign finance system. FECA was amended in 1974, following the Watergate scandal and the discovery of campaign finance abuses by Republican President Richard Nixon and his supporters. The legislation was again amended in 1976 and 1979.

The FECA had several key components. To promote transparency, the FECA required all candidates for federal office to submit itemized reports of expenditures and contributions over $200. To enforce campaign finance regulations, the legislation established a new federal agency, the Federal Election Commission (FEC). It also instituted a system of public financing for presidential elections, designed to level the playing field for candidates.

Most importantly for our purposes, the FECA banned direct contributions to federal candidates from all interest groups, except special organizations called political action committees, or PACs. PACs are political organizations that raise money to contribute to election campaigns. The FECA also imposed limits on how much money these PACs were allowed to contribute to federal campaigns. Specifically, it limited the amount PACs could contribute to $5,000 per candidate per election, with no limit on the overall total.

INTEREST GROUPS AND PACs

The architects of the FECA worried that money flowing directly from interest groups to candidates would encourage political corruption. They also worried that special interests with deep pockets would come to play a disproportionately powerful role in elections by controlling the purse strings of campaigns. That was the rationale for banning direct contributions to candidates from interest groups other than PACs.

Despite this ban, however, businesses, citizen groups, trade and professional associations, and other interest groups contribute millions to federal campaigns in every election cycle. This occurs because, even though interest groups are not allowed to contribute to candidates, they are allowed to establish PACs that do so on their behalf.

When an interest group sets up an affiliated PAC, it can solicit contributions from individuals, pool those contributions, and donate the funds to a candidate's campaign. However, none of the PAC's funds can come from the treasury of the parent organization, that is, the interest group itself. Instead, the PAC must have its own separate source of funds. Moreover, an affiliated PAC is allowed to solicit donations only from people associated with its parent organization. A citizen group, for example, can solicit only from its own members. A business can solicit only from its own shareholders and employees. However, anyone is allowed to donate to these PACS, including outside individuals, other PACs, political parties, and campaign committees.

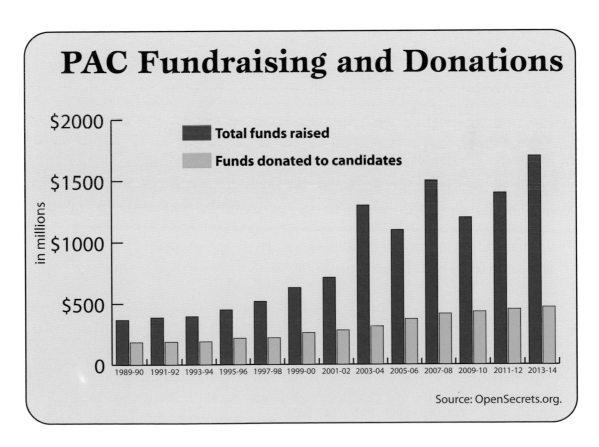

Top PACs Giving to Candidates in 2015

Honeywell International	$1,265,747
Lockheed Martin	$1,068,000
AT&T Inc.	$878,750
Northrop Grumman	$867,700
Credit Union National Association	$811,850
Blue Cross/Blue Shield	$763,350
Boeing Co.	$751,500
New York Life Insurance	$731,750
National Beer Wholesalers Association	$727,700
American Crystal Sugar	$723,500
PricewaterhouseCoopers	$723,099

Source: OpenSecrets.org

PAC Facts

Since the passage of FECA, PACs have come to play an increasingly big role in federal elections. In the mid-1970s, there were roughly 100 PACs active in the political arena. Today, there are about 4,000 PACs. The amount of money these groups are spending is also increasing dramatically. During the 2000 election, PACs spent about $260 million on candidate contributions. In the 2012 election, they spent $453 million.

Most PACs today are connected to specific corporations, labor unions, trade and professional associations, citizen groups, or other membership organizations. Increasingly, however, so-called nonconnected PACs have been growing in numbers. As the name suggests, nonconnected PACs are independent of any specific interest group. And unlike affiliated PACs, they are free to solicit money from anyone in the general public. That advantage is one reason why their numbers are growing. Both types of PACs, however, are subject to the same spending limits. The FEC also limits the size of contributions to PACs of either type to $5,000 per year from any given source.

HARD AND SOFT MONEY

Interest groups, through PACs, are an important source of money for candidates running for federal office. But because of FECA regulations, the total amount that a PAC can contribute to a given candidate is necessarily limited. Beginning in the 1990s, however, PACs began to take advantage of a loophole discovered in federal election laws. While the FECA places limits on contributions to candidates, campaign finance regulations place no limit on how much money PACs could give to state and local political parties for so-called "party-building activities." As long as the money was not spent on behalf of a specific candidate, PACs could spend as much as they wanted on such activities.

This type of unregulated spending is sometimes called soft money. Hard money, by contrast, refers to campaign contributions that are regulated by the FEC. During the1990s, PACs raised hundreds of millions of dollars through the soft money loophole. Soft money could be used for activities like publishing voter guides, organizing get-out-the-vote initiatives, or printing bumper stickers. Controversially, it could also be used to pay for ads that were designed to sway public opinion in federal elections. For example, a TV ad that showed a particular candidate and then told viewers to thank the candidate's party could be classified as a party-building expenditure, even though it was implicitly endorsing a specific candidate.

A well-known nonconnected PAC is Emily's List, dedicated to supporting pro-choice, female congressional candidates. Representing the opposite ideological platform is the National Right to Life PAC, a nonconnected PAC that works to elect pro-life candidates.

INTEREST GROUPS AND ELECTION ADS

A number of federal court cases in the 1990s, including *Maine Right to Life Committee v. FEC*, decided in 1996, spelled out the legal guidelines for acceptable ads. As long as an ad could be classified as advocating for an issue and not endorsing a candidate, it could be paid for with unregulated funds from an interest group's general treasury.

The courts explained the distinction between issue advocacy and candidate endorsement in terms of key action words, including vote for, elect, defeat, or vote against. Even if an ad depicted a candidate in a favorable or unfavorable light, it could be considered issue advocacy as long as it did not use any of these words or phrases.

In essence, this gave interest groups a way to campaign for candidates without having to resort to forming a PAC. Moreover, since this type of spending was not regulated by the FEC, interest groups could spend an unlimited amount of money on these ads. Not surprisingly, the amount of unregulated money interest groups were spending on ads skyrocketed. In the 1996 election alone, for example, the AFL-CIO spent $36 million on issue ads.

BIPARTISAN CAMPAIGN REFORM ACT OF 2002

In 2002, Congress passed new legislation to rein in interest groups and limit campaign spending. The Bipartisan Campaign Reform Act (BCRA), often called the McCain-Feingold Act after its Senate sponsors, largely banned the use of soft money in federal elections. It also established new standards for determining the difference between electioneering—campaigning for or against a specific candidate—and issue advocacy.

Specifically, the legislation defined an ad or other public broadcast as an "electioneering communication" if (1) it mentioned or featured a candidate and (2) it was aired within thirty days of a primary election or sixty days of a general election. In other words, an ad that met these conditions would be classified as "electioneering" and not "issue advocacy," even if it didn't use specific phrases such as vote for or vote against. This meant that any such ads could no longer be paid for with soft money out of an interest group's general treasury.

Marchers opposed to the U.S. Supreme Court's 2010 Citizens United *decision participate in a parade in Ypsilanti, Michigan. Many people believe that this ruling, as well as subsequent Supreme Court decisions such as* McCutcheon v. FEC *(2014), greatly weakened campaign finance laws and give the wealthy undue influence in the arena of political speech.*

Both of these restrictions on electioneering communications were struck down less than a decade later in the Supreme Court's 2010 *Citizens United* ruling.

CITIZENS UNITED V. FEC

During the 2008 election, a little-known conservative nonprofit, called Citizens United, used corporate funds to finance the production of a movie that was critical of Democratic presidential candidate Hillary Clinton. Although it was billed as a documentary, the movie resembled an extended attack ad. It was scheduled to air on cable TV right before the Democratic primary in January.

Under the terms set by the BCRA, this was a violation of campaign

Money and Elections

Elections in the United States cost an enormous amount of money, and the cost keeps going up. Every election cycle sets a new record for spending. During the 2000 election, candidates, political parties, and interest groups spent $3 billion trying to influence the outcome of the congressional and presidential races. In 2012, the total surpassed $6 billion. Candidates, political parties, and interest groups collectively spent more than $2.6 billion on the 2012 presidential race. They spent more than $3.6 billion on congressional races. Outside groups were responsible for almost a billion of that total amount, according to the Center for Responsive Politics. Millions more were spent by groups not required to disclose their funding sources. This spending frenzy was in large part the result of the sweeping changes ushered in by the landmark 2010 Supreme Court ruling in *Citizens United v. FEC*, which reversed a century of campaign finance laws.

During the 2012 presidential election, $1.14 billion was spent in support of the Republican candidate, Mitt Romney, including over $418 million raised by super PACs. The Democratic Party candidate, Barack Obama, benefitted from $964 million in campaign spending, including about $100 million raised and spent by super PACs.

finance laws on three counts. The movie targeted a specific candidate. It was partly funded with corporate cash. And it was set to air within thirty days of a primary election. Accordingly, the FEC blocked Citizens United from showing the movie. In response, Citizens United went to court, alleging that its free speech rights had been violated.

In a 5–4 decision, the Supreme Court ruled in January 2010 that it was unconstitutional to bar an interest group from using corporate or union general funds for electioneering activity. It also ruled that the thirty-day and the sixty-day time constraints were unconstitutional. Essentially, the High Court removed all restrictions on how much money corporations, unions, and nonprofits can spend on campaign ads designed to sway voters in federal elections. The only remaining restriction is that the ads must not be coordinated with any candidate or political party.

Not surprisingly, the election following the *Citizens United* ruling set a new record for interest group spending on ads. In the 2012 election, more than three million campaign ads were aired, costing almost $2 billion. Sixty percent of those ads were run by outside groups. A majority of those ads were negative in tone.

THE RISE OF THE SUPER PAC

Several lower court rulings and advisory opinions in the wake of *Citizens United* have expanded the scope of the ruling. One of the most important of these was *SpeechNow.org v. FEC*, decided in 2010. In this case, the U.S. District Court for the District of Columbia used the *Citizens United* decision as a precedent to strike down restrictions on contributions to so-called "independent expenditure" groups. Independent expenditures are funds spent on advocating for or against political candidates, as long as those actions are not coordinated with a candidate's campaign.

This ruling led to the creation of a new type of PAC that can both raise and spend unlimited amounts of money—the super PAC. A super PAC is different from a traditional PAC in two ways. First, unlike regular PACs, super PACs do not contribute to federal candidates. Their only purpose is to advertise for and against candidates in

Top Super PACs Funds Raised in 2015

Right To Rise USA	$103,167,845
Unintimidated PAC	$20,022,405
Conservative Solutions PAC	$16,057,755
Priorities USA Action	$15,654,457
Keep the Promise III	$15,000,000
Keep the Promise I	$11,007,096
America Leads	$11,003,304
Keep the Promise II	$10,000,000
Opportunity and Freedom I	$10,000,000
American Bridge 21st Century	$6,288,181
NextGen Climate Action	$5,257,112
Senate Leadership Fund	$4,923,500

Source: OpenSecrets.org

an election. Secondly, while the FECA sets limits on the amount that can be contributed to traditional PACs, super PACs are allowed to accept unlimited contributions. Because they can spend and raise unlimited amounts of money, super PACs are quickly becoming a growing force in elections. In the 2014 congressional elections, 1,360 super PACs reported raising almost $700 million and spending just under $350 million.

DARK MONEY

While super PACS can accept and spend unlimited amounts of money, they are still required to register with the FEC and to disclose their donors. Hence, they are still subject to a certain amount of oversight and transparency.

Another repercussion of *Citizens United*, however, has been the sharp increase in certain social welfare nonprofits, called 501(c)(4) groups after their classification in the tax code. Like super PACs, these groups are allowed to spend an unlimited amount of money on electioneering ads. Unlike super PACs, however, they are not required to disclose their donors.

These 501(c)(4) groups existed before the *Citizens United* ruling, but their sphere of action was limited. Previously, these groups could spend money only on issue ads—ads on general issues related to their cause. They were not allowed to directly advocate for the election or defeat of a candidate.

Thanks to the *Citizens United* ruling, however, these groups are now free to spend unlimited money on ads that explicitly endorse or reject candidates—without revealing the source of their funds. In effect, billionaires and big corporations can bankroll an advertising campaign behind the scenes without having their names publicly disclosed. This type of money is sometimes referred to as "dark money" or "shadow money" because the lack of disclosure makes it hard to trace. This is a growing concern among watchdog groups worried about transparency and oversight in government.

FREE SPEECH OR A THREAT TO DEMOCRACY?

Writing the Supreme Court's majority opinion in *Citizens United v. FEC*, Justice Anthony M. Kennedy argued that spending is a type of political speech protected by the First Amendment—even in the case of corporations. There is judicial precedent for this view. In its 1976

One of the most powerful 501(c)(4) nonprofits is Crossroads GPS, a spin-off of the conservative super PAC American Crossroads, founded by GOP strategist Karl Rove. Crossroads GPS raised $76 million in 2011, 90 percent of which came from undisclosed donors giving $1 million or more.

Buckley v. Valeo decision, the Supreme Court struck down limits on candidate campaign spending—like those included in the original FECA of 1971. The High Court argued in *Buckley* that these limits violated the free speech clause of the First Amendment.

Critics, however, warn that *Citizens United* has paved the way for wealthy special interests to influence elections to an unprecedented degree. President Obama said that the decision "strikes at our democracy itself."

The repercussions of the *Citizens United* ruling are still being understood, and campaign finance laws are still evolving. For now, however, most Americans seem to agree that the recent changes in federal election laws are troubling. In a May 2015 *New York Times*/CBS poll, 84 percent of respondents said that money has too much influence on American elections. Three-quarters agreed that there should be limits on campaign spending by outside groups and that contributions should be publicly disclosed.

Chapter 5

What the Future Holds

In 2011, Congress introduced two controversial bills aimed at curbing Internet piracy: the Protect Intellectual Property Act (PIPA) in the Senate and the Stop Online Piracy Act (SOPA) in the House of Representatives. Under these proposed laws, Internet sites that linked to copyrighted material would be punished with hefty fines and penalties. People who watched or listened to copyrighted online content without paying for it could be sent to prison for up to five years.

In Congress, SOPA and PIPA enjoyed broad bipartisan support. Outside of Congress, opinion was deeply divided. Supporters argued that the legislation was needed to protect intellectual property and enforce copyright law. Opponents warned that it was a threat to free speech.

Not surprisingly, a small army of lobbyists sprang into action on behalf of a long list of interest groups and corporations. The battle lines pitted major media companies against the computer and technology industry. Lobbyists for movie companies, television and cable networks, and the recording industry pressured Congress to pass the legislation. Internet companies campaigned against it. In total, more than

All together, groups like Wikipedia that opposed SOPA/PIPA shelled out $44 million lobbying against the legislation. Supporters, including Washington heavyweights like the U.S. Chamber of Commerce, spent a whopping $130 million lobbying in favor of SOPA/PIPA.

300 different companies and organizations lobbied for or against the legislation. Collectively, these groups spent more than $170 million.

AND THE WINNER IS . . .

By January 2012, the Senate bill had forty cosponsors and the House bill had thirty-one cosponsors. Passage of the legislation in both chambers of Congress looked certain. But six days before a key vote in the Senate was scheduled to take place, a massive online protest turned the political tide. On January 18, 2012, Wikipedia blacked out its site for twenty-four hours. Tens of thousands of other websites also partially or fully blocked access to their online content. Participants included not just major household names, like Reddit, Google,

YouTube, Mozilla, and WordPress, but also thousands of smaller websites. When visitors tried to access these sites, they instead encountered messages urging them to contact Congress to express their opposition to SOPA and PIPA.

In a single day, the blackout campaign generated about eight million phone calls to congressional offices, four million emails, and 10 million petition signatures. That very day, several cosponsors of the bills abruptly withdrew their support. Two days later, the legislation was shelved in both the Senate and the House.

CYBERSPACE VERSUS K STREET?

Many observers saw a broader lesson in this victory. To many, the SOPA/PIPA case showed that the power of the Internet was turning traditional models of lobbying on their head, replacing the ordinary channels of influence with new ways of mobilizing support.

After all, in the months leading up to the blackout campaign, Internet and tech companies had pursued traditional channels of lobbying without much success. Both supporters and opponents of the legislation sent roughly equal numbers of registered lobbyists to Capitol Hill. (According to the Center for Responsive Politics, 246 represented the computer and tech industry and 241 represented the television, music, and movie industries.) The Wikimedia Foundation registered to lobby for the first time. Google spent almost double the amount of money it had spent on lobbying the previous year. Yet months of traditional lobbying couldn't accomplish what a single one-day online protest did.

It is unlikely that online campaigns are going to replace traditional face-to-face lobbying. Clearly, however, the Internet and social media are changing how interest groups operate, the lobbying tactics they use, and the overall landscape of American politics in important ways.

Online tools are changing how interest groups lobby, including how they relate to members and how they pressure lawmakers. Social media are enabling new types of interest groups to play increasingly prominent roles in shaping policy debates. And they are empowering private citizens to push for change in politics in new ways.

DIRECT AND INDIRECT LOBBYING

Traditional lobbying involves direct contact with people inside government. For this reason, it is often called direct lobbying or inside lobbying. The people who might be targets of direct lobbying include federal and state legislators, their staff members, officials of the executive branch, committee members, representatives of federal or state agencies, and local officials—just about anyone in a policymaking role. Interest groups engage in direct lobbying by meeting personally with these policymakers, providing written communications and reports, and testifying at legislative hearings. Regardless of the means used, the goal of direct lobbying is to influence political decisions directly by contacting the policymakers themselves.

In addition to direct lobbying, interest groups also engage in what is sometimes called indirect lobbying, or outside lobbying. Indirect lobbying is aimed at people outside government—in other words, private citizens instead of people in positions of power. By directly engag-

Grassroots Change

The online petition site Change.org is used as a platform for campaigning by 100 million users. One of the most successful Change.org petitions was posted by the parents of seventeen-year-old Trayvon Martin, who was fatally shot in 2012 by neighborhood watch volunteer George Zimmerman. More than two million people signed the petition calling for local police to prosecute Zimmerman for the shooting. Zimmerman was eventually arrested and brought to trial, though he was acquitted of the murder charges.

Another notable petition targeted a U.S. Department of Agriculture (USDA) policy allowing school cafeterias to use pink slime—beef scraps and connective tissue treated with ammonia hydroxide—in school lunches. The petition got 200,000 signatures in nine days, and the USDA retracted its policy.

The rise of social media has created new channels for interest groups to spread their message to a wider audience, who in turn can put pressure on politicians to pass legislation that the interest group supports.

ing with private citizens, interest groups hope to indirectly influence policymakers.

Interest groups engage in various types of indirect lobbying. Sometimes the goal is simply to shape public opinion through informational campaigns and mailing lists. Other times the goal is to mobilize citizens to take action. For example, interest groups might organize rallies, demonstrations, letter-writing campaigns, petition drives, and other types of grassroots initiatives. The ultimate goal, however, is the same: to influence policymakers through pressure from ordinary citizens.

LOBBYING OVER THE WEB

Indirect lobbying is far from new. In the early 1900s, the Anti-Saloon League, a powerful Prohibition lobby, maintained a mailing list of 500,000 people in its crusade for temperance. In the 1960s and 1970s, civil rights groups helped to mobilize huge rallies against discriminatory laws.

Until relatively recently, however, interest groups had limited ways to reach prospective supporters. The digital revolution of the past few decades has made indirect lobbying much easier for interest groups. As a result, it is more commonly used as a lobbying technique than ever before. This has spawned a growing industry of indirect lobbying firms that specialize in helping interest groups mount indirect lobbying campaigns.

Interest groups reach huge numbers of people through email and

Black Lives Matter, a high-profile activist movement that crusades against police brutality, was born out of a Twitter hashtag.

blogs, plus Facebook, Twitter, and other social media. Websites, which are inexpensive to set up and easy to maintain, allow organizations to shape public opinion by providing information and news. They can generate instant activism by prompting visitors to click on links to contact elected officials about specific issues or campaigns.

Even corporations engage in indirect lobbying to shape people's attitudes and opinions. For example, ExxonMobil, one of the nation's largest oil companies, maintains a YouTube channel with slickly produced videos on dozens of topics. Among them are videos on the controversial practice of hydraulic fracturing, or "fracking," which has been criticized by environmentalists and many health advocates as bad for the environment and for human health.

NETROOTS AND NEW MEDIA

New media—a term referring to digital technologies, such as the Internet—are giving long-established interest groups more effective tools for indirect lobbying. It has also led to the emergence of new types of interest groups that offer a changing model for political involvement.

Traditionally, the model for a successful interest group was the large, well-funded group with a national headquarters based in Washington, D.C. and a large, in-house lobbying and policy staff. In the past fifteen years or so, however, a number of highly successful web-based organizations have been established. These groups are sometimes called "netroots"—a combination of "Internet" and "grass-roots." As the name suggests, they rely on email, websites, and social media to communicate their message and mobilize support.

While these new organizations have relatively few full-time staff, they have memberships in the millions. One of the oldest of these netroots organizations is MoveOn.org, founded in 1998. It has eight million members. Organizing for Action, founded in 2013, has thirteen million members.

Increasingly, these groups are showing that having a large budget for lobbying may be less important than having a visible online presence and a large membership list.

POWER TO THE PEOPLE

Web tools are effective in large part because they are inexpensive to use, they can reach huge numbers of people at one time, and they can generate a rapid response. For these same reasons, the Internet is also proving to be a powerful means for private citizens to take policy battles into their own hands.

Returning to the case of the Sandy Hook Elementary School shooting, cited in chapter one, consider just one example of how private citizens are harnessing the power of the Internet to have a say in the political process. In 2012, Shannon Watts was a stay-at-home mom in Indiana with no background in politics or community organizing. Shocked and saddened by the shooting at the elementary school in Newtown, Connecticut, Watts started a Facebook group to express her frustrations about the lack of effective gun control in the United States.

The very first day, the group—Moms Demand Action for Gun Sense in America—got hundreds of "likes." By the end of the first week, that number had swelled to the thousands. Today, it has over 400,000 likes and has grown into a national organization with 130,000 members and chapters in all fifty states. The group has successfully lobbied a number of national chains, including Target and Chipotle, to ban customers from openly carrying firearms in their stores, even in states where it is legal to do so.

PROMISE AND PERIL

Facebook, Twitter, and other social media platforms will never replace lobbyists and traditional interest groups in American politics. Nonetheless, it is clear that the Internet is opening up new channels of influence and new ways of participating in policy debates. It may even help to usher in positive changes in the institution of lobbying.

As we saw in chapter 2, many Americans have a cynical view of lobbyists and special-interest groups. In large part, this cynicism stems from the perception that these groups can use their money and clout to bias the political system. The Internet, however, may have an equalizing effect, serving to level the playing field to some degree. Anyone

Protesters denounce the influence of money in the American political system and encourage reform during an event in New York City. Many experts believe that the 2016 presidential campaign will set records for campaign fundraising and spending, with a total possibly exceeding $5 billion.

can start an online petition or a Facebook group for free.

As we saw in chapter 3, concern about transparency and oversight has been the driving force behind attempts to regulate lobbying. In this respect, too, the Internet plays a positive role by putting data at the fingertips of citizens and watchdog groups.

At the same time, however, these social media platforms may be problematic. False or distorted information can spread rapidly over the Internet. Phony online campaigns are easy to pull off. Oversight is important both offline and online. Yet, currently, federal law does not regulate online campaigning or mandate the disclosure of indirect lobbying activities.

INTO THE FUTURE

Interest groups and lobbyists have helped to shape American politics throughout the nation's history. In turn, the changes of the day—from political scandals to new legislation to new forms of technology—have shaped how lobbyists and interest groups function.

It remains to be seen what changes the twenty-first century will bring. It is clear, however, that the Internet will play a key role in this change. It is also certain that lobbyists and interest groups will remain an important part of America's political landscape in the future.

Chapter Notes

p. 6   "gun lobby and its allies . . .": Barack Obama, "Obama's Remarks After Senate Gun Votes," *New York Times* (April 17, 2013). http://www.nytimes.com/2013/04/18/us/politics/obamas-remarks-after-senate-gun votes.html?_r = 0&gwh = 0CFAAB140C11CFF2A30E1DA12 D9872AA&gwt = pay.

p. 6   "a victory for partisanship . . .": Mitch McConnell, quoted in Coral Davenport, "Senate Fails to Override Obama's Keystone Pipeline Veto," *New York Times* (March 4, 2015). http://www.nytimes.com/2015/03/05/us/senate-fails-to-override-obamas-keystone-pipeline-veto.html?_r = 0.

p. 6   "a few special interests . . .": Chuck Schumer, quoted in Joseph Tanfani, "Obama Veto of Keystone Pipeline Would Stick, Top Democrat Says," *Los Angeles Times* (January 4, 2015). http://www.latimes.com/nation/politics/politicsnow/la-pn-keystone-20150104-story.html.

p. 6   "We have come to take . . .": Rand Paul, quoted in Katie Zezima and Robert Costa, "Rand Paul Launches 2016 White House Bid," *Washington Post* (April 7, 2015). http://www.washingtonpost.com/news/post-politics/wp/2015/04/07/rand-paul-set-to-announce-presidential-run/.

p. 9   "I've never been entirely comfortable,": Barack Obama, *The Audacity of Hope* (New York: Three Rivers Press, 2006), p. 116.

p. 12   "Congress shall make no law . . .": First Amendment of the Constitution of the United States, online text. http://www.archives.gov/exhibits/charters/constitution_transcript.html.

p. 12   "Most elected officials . . .": Pew Research Center, "Beyond Distrust: How Americans View Their Government," November 23, 2015. http://www.people-press.org/2015/11/23/beyond-distrust-how-americans-view-their-government/

p. 12   "just about always," Ibid.

p. 14   "advocacy explosion . . .": David Knoke, "Associations and Interest Groups," *Annual Review of Sociology* 12 (1986): 15.

p. 17   "united and actuated by some common,": James Madison, Federalist Paper No. 10, 1787. http://thomas.loc.gov/home/histdox/fed_10.html.

p. 17   "worse than the disease," Ibid.

p. 21   "Congress has always had,": Robert C. Byrd, reprinted in *Addresses on the History of the United States Senate, 1789–1989* (Washington, D.C.: U.S. Government Printing Office, 1991), p. 508.

p. 24   "principal purpose," Federal Regulation of Lobbying Act of 1946 (2 U.S. Code §§ 261). https://www.law.cornell.edu/uscode/text/2/261

p. 44   "strikes at our democracy itself . . .": Barack Obama, quoted in Sheryl Gay Stolberg, "Obama Turns Up Heat Over Ruling on Campaign Spending," *New York Times* (January 23, 2010). http://www.nytimes.com/2010/01/24/us/politics/24address.html?_r = 0.

Chronology

1787 Founding father James Madison writes about the threat of factions, or interest groups, in the Federalist Papers.

1792 Veterans of the Continental Army hire a former Revolutionary War officer named William Hull to lobby the newly formed Congress for more money. This is the earliest recorded act of lobbying in the United States.

1876 The U.S. House of Representatives passes a resolution requiring lobbyists to register with the clerk of the House, but only for that session of Congress.

1907 The Tillman Act bans corporations and banks from making direct contributions to candidates for federal office.

1946 Congress passes the first comprehensive federal lobbying law, the Federal Regulation of Lobbying Act of 1946.

1947 The Taft-Hartley Act of 1947 bans labor unions from making direct contributions to candidates for federal election.

1971 Congress passes the Federal Election Campaign Act (FECA), regulating the federal campaign finance system. Amendments to the FECA follow in 1974, 1976, and 1979.

1995 President Bill Clinton signs the Lobbying Disclosure Act into law, aimed at promoting a greater degree of transparency and accountability in federal lobbying practices.

2002 Congress passes the Bipartisan Campaign Reform Act, often called the McCain-Feingold Act, largely banning the use of soft money in federal elections. McCain-Feingold also sets new standards for electioneering ads.

2006 High-powered Washington lobbyist Jack Abramoff pleads guilty to fraud, corruption, and conspiracy, prompting Congress to revamp federal lobbying regulations.

2007 Congress passes the Honest Leadership and Open Government Act, trying to eliminate some of the loopholes in the Lobbying Disclosure Act of 1995.

2009 The day after his inauguration, President Obama issues an executive order aimed at strengthening ethics regulations at the executive level of government.

2010 In *Citizens United v. Federal Election Commission*, the Supreme Court strikes down limits on corporate and union election spending, reversing a century of legal precedent. *SpeechNow.org v. Federal Election Commission* uses the *Citizens United* ruling as a precedent and leads to the creation of the super PAC—a type of political action committee that can raise and spend unlimited amounts of money.

2012 The first federal election after the *Citizens United* ruling sets a record as the most expensive election in history. Large amounts of money are spent by groups that do not disclose their donors.

Glossary

affiliated—closely associated with something or someone else; connected or related.

appease—to make people pleased or to make them less angry than they might otherwise be; to give in to a group's demands in order to pacify them.

bipartisan—agreement or cooperation between two political parties that have opposing policies and ideological beliefs.

compliance—the act of complying to something, or obeying.

constituent—a voter represented by an elected official.

disclose—to reveal or make known.

disincentive—a factor that discourages people from doing something.

earmark—in legislation passed by Congress, this is a directive that says funds should be spent for a particular project.

expenditure—money that is spent.

FEC—the Federal Election Commission, which oversees and enforces federal election laws and acts.

gridlock—a situation in which no progress or movement is possible.

interest group—an organized group that tries to influence the government to adopt certain policies or measures that favor or help a business or cause affiliated with the group.

lobbyist—someone who is hired by a business or a cause to persuade legislators to support that business or cause.

loophole—a small gap that allows people to get out of something, such as following a regulation or law.

lucrative—profitable; producing or involving great wealth.

PAC—a political action committee formed in support of candidates and specific issues.

paradox—something that has qualities that seem to contradict each other.

pharmaceutical—relating to medicinal drugs.

precedent—something done or said earlier that can be used as an example or rule for the future.

proliferate—to grow in number or increase rapidly.

repercussion—a consequence or result of something.

super PAC—a political action committee that can raise unlimited funds from contributors and is not limited in how much money it can spend in support of a candidate as long as there is no coordination between the candidate's official campaign and the super PAC.

unprecedented—never done or experienced before.

Further Reading

Archer, Jules. *Special Interests: How Lobbyists Influence Legislation.* Brookfield, CT: Millbrook Press, 1997.

Donovan, Sandra. *Special Interests: From Lobbyists to Campaign Funding.* Minneapolis: Lerner Publications Company, 2016.

Duignan, Brian. *Political Parties, Interest Groups, and Elections.* New York: Britannica Educational Publishing, 2012.

Handlin, Amy. *Dirty Deals? An Encyclopedia of Lobbying, Political Influence, and Corruption.* Santa Barbara, Calif.: ABC-CLIO, 2014.

Horn, Geoffrey M. *Political Parties, Interest Groups, and the Media.* Milwaukee: World Almanac Library, 2004. Print.

Sandak, Cass R. *Lobbying.* New York: Twenty-First Century Books, 1995.

Internet Resources

http://ballotpedia.org

This fully searchable online encyclopedia is a comprehensive resource on American politics and elections.

http://www.publicintegrity.org

The "Politics" section of this nonprofit investigative news organization reports on campaign donations, lobbying, and special-interest groups.

http://www.opensecrets.org

The Center for Responsive Politics is a nonpartisan, nonprofit research group advocating for transparency and accountability in government.

http://www.fec.gov

The Federal Election Commission maintains a searchable database of campaign finance data, plus information about relevant legislation, policy statements, and advisory opinions.

http://reporting.sunlightfoundation.com/lobbying

The Sunlight Foundation's website includes data, policy analyses, and investigative reporting on topics ranging from campaign finance to lobbying to government spending.

Index

Numbers in **bold italic** refer to captions.

About the Author

Elisabeth Herschbach is former philosophy teacher with a Ph.D. from the University of Pennsylvania. She currently works as an editor, writer, and translator in Maryland, where she lives with her husband, Michael, and their son, Alexander. Her books for a middle-school audience include *Lower Plains: Kansas, Nebraska* (Mason Crest, 2015) and *Global Inequalities and the Fair Trade Movement* (Mason Crest, 2016). In 2009, Elisabeth received the Constantinides Memorial Translation prize from the Modern Greek Studies Association for her translation of a 1938 novel by the Greek writer Kosmas Politis.

PHOTO CREDITS: Carlos Barria / Reuters / Landov: 28; Library of Congress: 24; OTTN Publishing: 15, 35; used under license from Shutterstock, Inc.: 1, 4, 20, 22; Atomazul / Shutterstock.com: 8; Featureflash / Shutterstock.com: 31; Jose Gil / Shutterstock.com: 16; Glynnis Jones / Shutterstock.com: 11; A. Katz / Shutterstock.com: 50, 53; Susan Montgomery / Shutterstock.com: 39; Brent Olson / Shutterstock.com: 19; Charlotte Purdy / Shutterstock.com: 40 (right); Betto Rodrigues / Shutterstock.com: 7; Rena Schild / Shutterstock.com: 27 (bottom); Annette Shaff / Shutterstock.com: 46; Joseph Sohm / Shutterstock.com: 30, 40 (left); Twin Design / Shutterstock.com: 49; U.S. Senate collection: 25, 27 (top). Front cover: used under license from Shutterstock, Inc. (left; bottom right); Joseph Sohm / Shutterstock.com (top right). Back cover: used under license from Shutterstock, Inc.